I0605177

Glass Frog

by Julie Murray

Abdo Kids Jumbo is an Imprint of Abdo Kids
abdobooks.com

abdobooks.com

Published by Abdo Kids, a division of ABDO, P.O. Box 398166, Minneapolis, Minnesota 55439.

Printed in the United States of America, North Mankato, Minnesota.

102024

012025

Photo Credits: Alamy, Getty Images, Minden Pictures, Shutterstock

Production Contributors: Teddy Borth, Jennie Forsberg, Grace Hansen
Design Contributors: Victoria Bates, Candice Keimig

Library of Congress Control Number: 2024936607

Publisher's Cataloging-in-Publication Data

Names: Murray, Julie, author.

Title: Glass frog / by Julie Murray

Description: Minneapolis, Minnesota : Abdo Kids, 2025 | Series: Unusual animals | Includes online resources and index.

Identifiers: ISBN 9798384903055 (lib. bdg.) | ISBN 9798384903758 (ebook) | ISBN 9798384904106 (Read-to-me ebook)

Subjects: LCSH: Glass frogs (Amphibians)--Juvenile literature. | Frogs--Juvenile literature. | Amphibians--Juvenile literature. | Rain forest animals--Juvenile literature. | Wildlife--Juvenile literature. | Enigmas--Juvenile literature.

Classification: DDC 597.89--dc23

Table of Contents

Glass Frog

Glass frogs are found in southern Mexico, Central America, and South America. There are more than 150 different **species**.

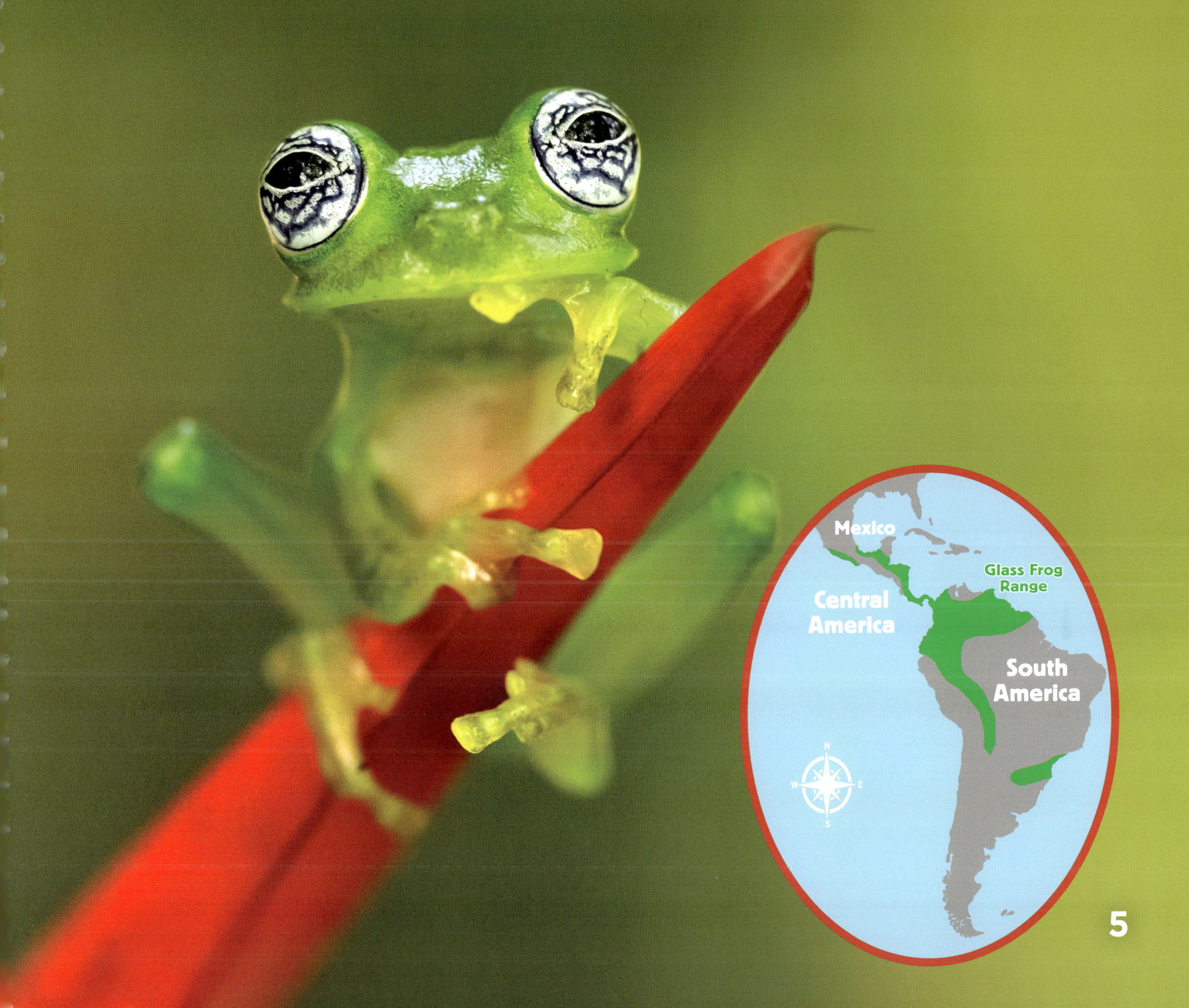
Mexico
Glass Frog
Range
Central
America
South
America
N
W
E
S

Glass frogs live in **humid** rainforests and tropical lowland areas. They stay up in trees. They come down during **mating** season.

Glass frogs are unusual. The skin on their bellies is see-through! They also have bulging eyes with black **pupils**.

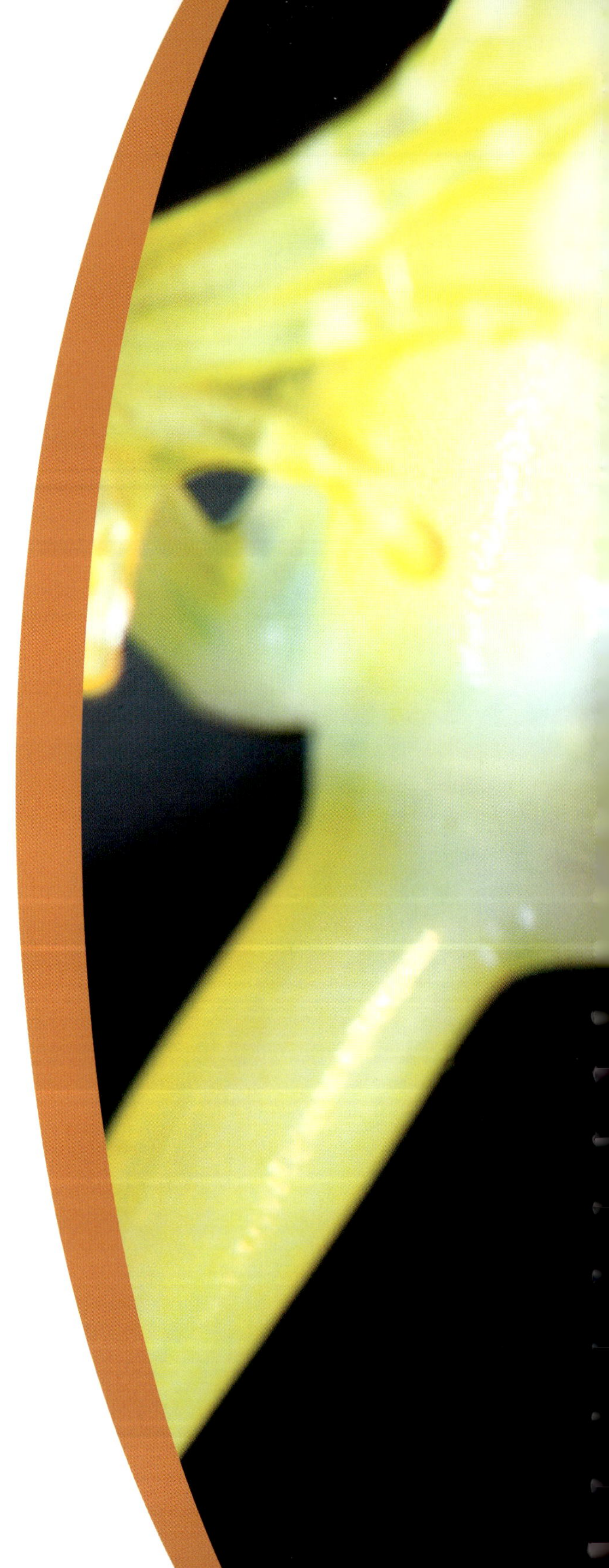

Body

Glass frogs are small. Adults are about 1 inch (2.5 cm) long. Most glass frogs have bright green backs. Some have yellow and black spots. Others are white with egg-shaped markings.

Glass frogs have yellow suction pads on their toes. These help them climb trees.

Viewing glass frogs from underneath is special. Their heart, intestines, and bones can be seen through their skin!

Food

Glass frogs like to eat ants, crickets, and spiders. Unlike most frogs, glass frogs have short tongues! Hunting insects is harder to do.

Cricket

Baby Glass Frogs

Female glass frogs lay about 35 eggs at a time. The eggs are laid carefully on leaves that hang over water.

Male glass frogs guard the eggs. They often lay on top of the eggs. Once the eggs hatch, the tadpoles fall into the water below. Soon they will grow into adult frogs!

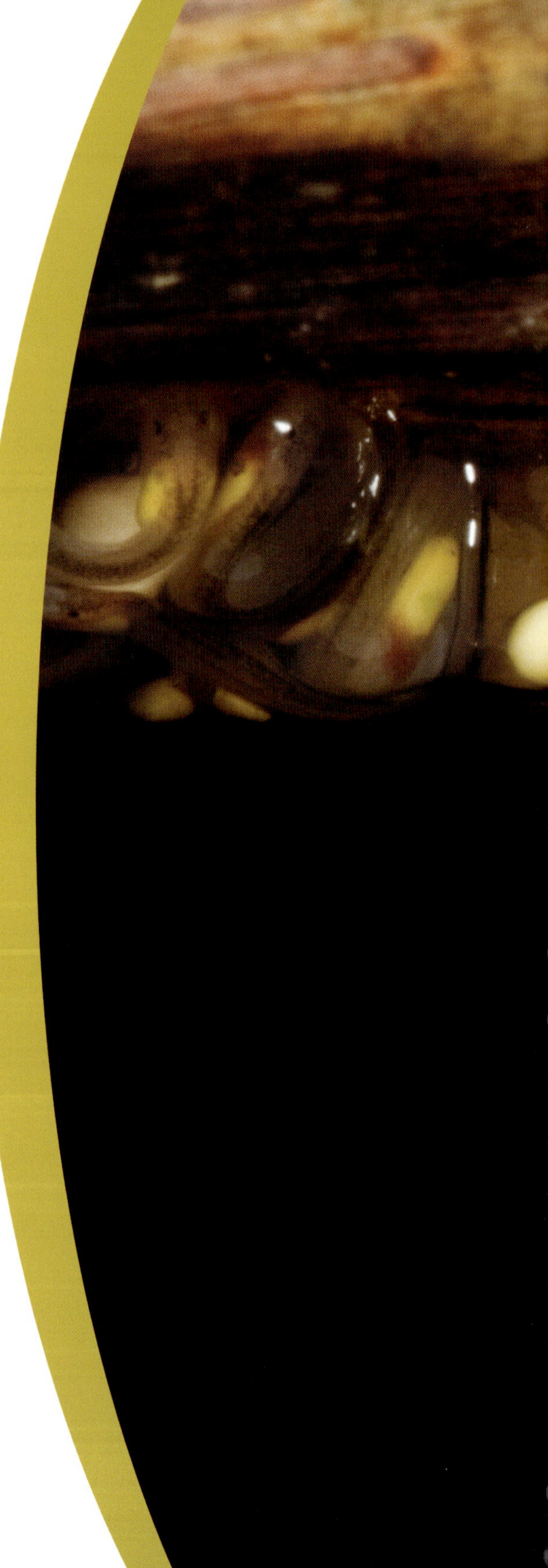

More Facts

- Glass frogs are strong jumpers. They can jump up to 10 feet (3 m)!
- Glass frogs live for 10 to 14 years in the wild.
- Glass frogs make a high-pitched whistling sound to attract a mate.

Glossary

humid - moist or muggy.

mating - coming together to have offspring.

pupil - the small, dark opening in the center of the eye. Light passes through the pupil into the eye.

species - a group of living things that look alike and can have young together.

Index